UNENDING
BLUES

Charles Simic

UNENDING
BLUES

Poems

A HARVEST BOOK
HARCOURT BRACE & COMPANY

San Diego   New York   London

Requests for permission to make copies of
any part of the work should be mailed to:
Permissions Department, Harcourt Brace & Company,
6277 Sea Harbor Drive, Orlando, Florida 32887-6777.

Some of these poems have previously appeared
in the following periodicals, to whose editors
grateful acknowledgment is made:
TriQuarterly, *Blue Fish*, the *Kenyon Review*,
Harvard Magazine, the *Missouri Review*, *Field*,
American Poetry Review, the *Georgia Review*,
the *Yale Review*, the *Seneca Review*, the *Iowa Review*,
Poetry, and the *Pushcart Prize X: Best of the Small Presses*.
The poem "Early Evening Algebra" originally appeared
in the *New Yorker*.

Library of Congress Cataloging-in-Publication Data
Simic, Charles, 1938–
    Unending blues.
    "A Harvest book."
    I. Title.
PS3569.I4725U55 1986   811'.54   86-9800
ISBN 0-15-192830-4
ISBN 0-15-692831-0 (pbk.)

Designed by Michael Farmer
Printed in the United States of America
First Harvest edition 1986
G F E D C

Contents

THREE

One

December

It snows
and still the derelicts
go
carrying sandwich boards—

one proclaiming
the end of the world
the other
the rates of a local barbershop

The Marvels of the City

FOR BATA

I went down the tree-lined street of false gods
The cobbled street of two wise monkeys
The street of roasted nightingales
The small twisted street of the insomniacs
The street of those who feather their beds

That's right—the street of the dog's metaphysics
The dark alley of the Emperor's favorite barber
With its fountain and stone lion
The closed shutters on the street of the hundred-
    year-old harlot
The flag-bedecked courthouses and banks
On the square of the betrayed revolution

Here at last I thought feeling a rush of blood
The street of eternal recurrence and its proof
The tavern at the sign of the Pig and
    Seraphim
Erudite salamanders sipping wine of arctic vintage
Hamlet's wine the wine of stargazers
Loveless couples the wine of idiot savants

We are solely of the mind said one
Beyond Good and Evil said another
But the waiters black hair growing out of their
    ears
Just took our orders and said nothing

The Implements of Augury

FOR LJUBINKA

Something like an empty chair and table
In a fortune-teller's storefront.
The Madame herself withdrawn from view,
Leaving us the dimly lit lampshade . . .

Most certainly, bequeathing to our care:
The empty street, the late hour,
The flowered tablecloth with tassels,
A neat pack of cards face down

In a huge nightbound city
Of many churches, hospitals,
Prisons and high tribunals
All equally deserted now.

The Madame herself withdrawn from view.
The cards as they were. The lampshade
With its flying mermaids and dragons,
The smiling mermaids, the fire-spitting dragons.

Toward Nightfall

FOR DON AND JANE

The weight of tragic events
On everyone's back,
Just as tragedy
In the proper Greek sense
Was thought impossible
To compose in our day.

There were scaffolds,
Makeshift stages,
Puny figures on them,
Like small indistinct animals
Caught in the headlights
Crossing the road way ahead,

In the gray twilight
That went on hesitating
On the verge of a huge
Starless autumn night.
One could've been in
The back of an open truck
Hunkering because of
The speed and chill.

One could've been walking
With a sidelong glance
At the many troubling shapes
The bare trees made—
Like those about to shriek,

But finding themselves unable
To utter a word now.

One could've been in
One of these dying mill towns
Inside a small dim grocery
When the news broke.
One would've drawn near the radio
With the one many months pregnant
Who serves there at that hour.

Was there a smell of
Spilled blood in the air,
Or was it that other,
Much finer scent—of fear,
The fear of approaching death
One met on the empty street?

Monsters on movie posters, too,
Prominently displayed.
Then, six factory girls,
Arm in arm, laughing
As if they've been drinking.
At the very least, one
Could've been one of them.

The one with a mouth
Painted bright red,
Who feels out of sorts,
For no reason, very pale,
And so, excusing herself,
Vanishes where it says:
Rooms for Rent,
And immediately goes to bed,
Fully dressed, only

To lie with eyes open,
Trembling, despite the covers.
It's just a bad chill,
She keeps telling herself
Not having seen the papers
Which the landlord has the dog
Bring from the front porch.

The old man never learned
To read well, and so
Reads on in that half-whisper,
And in that half-light
Verging on the dark,
About that day's tragedies
Which supposedly are not
Tragedies in the absence of
Figures endowed with
Classic nobility of soul.

Early Evening Algebra

The madwoman went marking X's
With a piece of school chalk
On the backs of unsuspecting
Hand-holding, homebound couples.

It was winter. It was dark already.
One could not see her face
Bundled up as she was and furtive.
She went as if wind-swept, as if crow-winged.

The chalk must have been given to her by a child.
One kept looking for him in the crowd,
Expecting him to be very pale, very serious,
With a chip of black slate in his pocket.

William and Cynthia

Says she'll take him to the Museum
Of Dead Ideas and Emotions.
Wonders that he hasn't been there yet.
Says it looks like a Federal courthouse
With its many steps and massive columns.

Apparently not many people go there
On such drizzly gray afternoons.
Says even she gets afraid
In the large empty exhibition halls
With monstrous ideas in glass cases,
Naked emotions on stone pedestals
In classically provocative poses.

Says she doesn't understand why he claims
All that reminds him of a country fair.
Admits there's a lot of old dust
And the daylight is the color of sepia,
Just like on this picture postcard
With its two lovers chastely embracing
Against a painted cardboard sunset.

Ever So Tragic

Heart—as in Latin popsongs
Blaring from the poolhall radio.
The air had thickened, the evening air.
He took off his white shirt.
The heart, one could mark it
With lipstick on a bare chest,
The way firing-squad commanders mark it.

He was reading in the papers
About the artificial heart.
The same plastic they use for wind-up toys,
She thought. More likely
Like an old wheelbarrow to push:
Heart of stone, knife-grinder's
Stone . . .
          Later
It was raining and they got into bed.
O desire, O futile hope, O sighs!
In coal miner's pit and lantern:
The heart, the bright red heart . . .

Didn't the blind man just call
His little dog that?

Hearts make haste, hasten on!

For the Sake of Amelia

Tending a cliff-hanging Grand Hotel
In a country ravaged by civil war.
My heart as its only bellhop.
My brain as its Chinese cook.

It's a run-down seaside place
With a row of gutted limousines out front,
Monkeys and fighting cocks in the great ballroom,
Potted palm trees grown wild to the ceilings.

Amelia surrounded by her beaus and fortune-
        tellers,
Painting her eyelashes and lips blue
In the hour of dusk with the open sea beyond,
The long empty beaches, the tide's shimmer . . .

She pleading with me to check the ledgers,
Find out if Lenin stayed here once,
Buster Keaton, Nathaniel Hawthorne,
St. Bernard of Clairvaux, who wrote on love?

A hotel in which one tangos to a silence
Which has the look of cypresses in silent
        films . . .
In which children confide to imaginary
        friends . . .
In which pages of an important letter are
        flying . . .

But now a buzz from the suite with mirrors.
Amelia in the nude, black cotton over her eyes.

It seems there's a fly
On the tip of her lover's Roman nose.

Night of distant guns, distant and comfortable.
I am coming with a flyswatter on a silver tray.
Ah the Turkish delights!
And the Mask of Tragedy over her pubic hair.

Avenue of the Americas

FOR BILL AND BEV

A cat and a mouse were lapping milk
From the same saucer
For the benefit of the lunch-hour crowd.

The owner of the pair
Had a tucked sleeve in place of a right arm
And no teeth despite his youth.

He kept smiling and bowing deeply
In the manner of a servant
Of a haughty and severe master.

History

Men and women with kick-me signs on their
    backs.
Let's suppose he was sad and she was upset.
They got over it. The spring day bore a semblance
    to what they hoped.
Then came History. He was arrested and shot.

Do they speak in heroic couplets as he's dragged
    away looking over his shoulder?
A few words for that park statue with pigeons
    on it?
More likely she wipes her eyes and nose with a
    sleeve,
Asks for a stiff drink, takes her place in the
    breadline.

Then the children die of hunger, one by one.
Of course, there are too many such cases for
    anyone to be underlining them with a red
    pencil.
Plus, the propensity of widows to flaunt their
    widowhood:
Coarse pubic hair, much-bitten breasts.

History loves to see women cry, she whispers.
Their death makes Art, he shouts, naked.
How pretty are the coffins and instruments of
    torture
In the Museum on the day of free admission to
    the public!

For the Lovers of the Absolute

A skinny arm thrown under
Her short-cropped head;
Then the penciled eyebrows,
Lips of a very serious child.

Naked and stretching herself
As if still convulsed
By passionate embraces—
Knees raised, thighs open
For a peek at the luxurious
Growth of black curls,

Glistening. The man by her side
With eyes shut. Broad chest,
Adam's apple rising evenly.
Already asleep—mouth open.
One long finely tapered hand
Cupping his sex as if in pain.

Still, instead of snores she hears
The distant artillery fire
That makes the blinds rattle
Ever so slightly; her breasts
Turn that ugly gooseflesh color—
And then she's fast asleep herself.

On Thursday

I met the mortician on the street.
He embraced me. Thus we strolled to the corner
Where a fallen angel runs a tavern.
Its only waitress is my great love

Who will die young and by her own hand.
It will be spring, I told the mortician
Over a drink, told him several times.
He promised to show her naked to me one last
        time.

The angel was combing his blond wig
When a lamb dragging a heavy chain
Entered from the street. Tongue-tied
We waited for its mother to call it back.

My love was sitting on the mortician's knees
Arms thrown around his fat neck.
She kept swaying and brushing her breasts
Against his lips that went on opening wider and
        wider.

Such teeth I once saw on a child reared by wolves,
        someone said—
And, truly, there was a hot band playing.
The angel had his eyes on two soldiers dancing
        together.
The roasting lamb began to smell of rosemary.

The Worm of Conscience

Nightcrawler, is it time?

My head stuffed with yellowed pages
As if there were a courtroom nearby
And these its stacked-up documents.

Did you crawl out of the black heart of the
        prosecuting attorney?
Tunneling through the ornate signature of the
        judgment
On a special errand
Over the morgue reports and orphans' petitions.

Maker of labyrinths, is that it?
Contorting myself to overtake you.

Little white lies in a cage—
I intend to feed you to.

At the Night Court

You've combed yourself carefully,
Your Honor, with a small fine-tooth comb
You then cleverly concealed
Before making your entrance
In the splendor of your black robes.

The comb tucked inside a handkerchief
Scented with the extract of dead roses—
While you took your high seat
Sternly eyeing each of the accused
In the hush of the empty courtroom.

The dark curly hairs in the comb
Did not come from your graying head.
One of the cleaning women used it on herself
While you dozed off in your chambers
Half undressed because of the heat.

The black comb in the pocket over the heart,
You feel it tremble just as ours do
When they ready themselves to make music
Lacking only the paper you're signing,
By the looks of it, with eyes closed.

TWO

Dark Farmhouses

Windy evening,
Chinablue snow,
The old people are shivering
In their kitchens.

Truck without lights
Idling on the highway,
Is it a driver you require?
Wait a bit.

There's coal to load up,
A widow's sack of coal.

Is it a shovel you need?
Idle on,
A shovel will come by and by
Over the darkening plain.

A shovel,
And a spade.

Wherein Obscurely

On the road with billowing poplars,
In a country flat and desolate
To the far-off gray horizon, wherein obscurely,
A man and a woman went on foot,

Each carrying a small suitcase.
They were tired and had taken off
Their shoes and were walking on
Their toes, staring straight ahead.

Every time a car passed fast,
As they're wont to on such a stretch of
Road, empty as the crow flies,
How quickly they were gone—

The cars, I mean, and then the drizzle
That brought on the early evening,
Little by little, and hardly a light
Anywhere, and then not even that.

The Animal Trainer

I endured your gaze, master.
You were old and diminutive,
No longer shadowed by the blonde
Carrying the long whip.

It happened that a small bird
Alighted in a tree just then
Making up its mind
Whether to fly off or sing.

If I could snip its tongue
(You whispered), it would talk,
Plead to have a mirror and a bell
Put in its cage on Sundays.

As for me, it was clear,
I couldn't be taught anything,
Though a daily whipping
Would do me a world of good.

Popular Mechanics

The enormous engineering problems
You'll encounter by attempting to crucify yourself
Without helpers, pulleys, cogwheels,
And other clever mechanical contrivances—

In a small, bare, white room,
With only a loose-legged chair
To reach the height of the ceiling—
Only a shoe to beat the nails in.

Not to mention being naked for the occasion—
So that each rib and muscle shows.
Your left hand already spiked in,
Only the right to wipe the sweat with,

To help yourself to a butt
From the overflowed ashtray,
You won't quite manage to light—
And the night coming, the whiz night.

Muttering Perhaps, or Humming

I avidly read the classics
In a dirty little mill town,
The weather of the soul turning
Bitter. My brain, it seemed,

Constructed by Daedalus, I was
Lost hopelessly at the entrance
Of the maze while spooning
My bowl of breakfast cereal

In company of night watchmen,
High school dropouts thinking of
A career in the army. The gods
Looked like hairdressers for dead

Lovers. I made myself learn
Their names so I could rename
All my neighbors, even the ugly
Ones biting on bad cigars.

Afternoons I lazed with a woman
In a place with shades drawn.
We played cards in the nude, made
Love on all fours. I wanted some

Herodotus to remember us briefly
Before describing the high and mighty
Dining on nightingale tongues
Chez the Gorgons, the fashionable ones.

In the Alley

You, with an earring, who diligently
Tattoo a bird of paradise
On the scrawny chest of a young sailor,
Didn't you notice it kept on snowing

Far into the night? While you labored
Over the colorful and ornate plumage
Of the exotic bird, and the beardless one
Sat shivering naked to the waist.

The great towers of Banking and Industry
Theatrically veiled and dimmed . . .
The grated shopwindows with their mannequins
Heads inclined as if overhearing things . . .

The heavy mirror you're tilting
For an admiring view
Of the spread wings, the wide-open beak
Triumphant—where the heart was!

Department of Public Monuments

If Justice and Liberty
Can be raised to pedestals,
Why not History?

It could be that fat woman
In faded overalls
Outside a house trailer
On a muddy road to some place called Pittsfield
    or Babylon.

She draws the magic circle
So the chickens can't get out,
Then she hobbles to the kitchen
For the knife and pail.

Today she's back carrying
A sack of yellow corn.
You can hear the hens cluck,
The dogs rattle their chains.

A Place in the Country

How well these dogs and their fleas
Know me and my black hat, not to mention
That fine collection of deathbeds upstairs.
How happy must be the frying pan

I take off its antique wrought-iron hook,
And the spoons which spent so much time
In the dark drawer, so that now
They look at the world wild-eyed.

They like me even better when
I eat too much and stretch on the floor.
Even the dust knows me then, and of course,
The wedding photographs on the wall.

What wouldn't they do for me, these long-
         departed couples!
At times the grandmothers strip naked,
And the men weep since we are at home,
And the fire is roaring in the stove,

While up above in what are still called the
         heavens,
There's our own chimney smoke
Like an old-time coachman's whip
For both the good and the bad angels.

The Fly

He was writing the History of Optimism
In Time of Madness. It was raining.
One of the local butcher's largest
Carrion fanciers kept pestering him.

There was a cat too watching the fly,
And a gouty-footed old woman
In a dirty bathrobe and frayed slippers
Bringing in a cup of pale tea.

With many sighs and long pauses
He found a bit of blue sky on the day of the
      Massacre of the Innocents.
He found a couple of lovers,
A meadow strewn with yellow flowers. . . .

But he couldn't go on. . . . O blue-winged,
      shivering one, he whispered.
Some days it's like using a white cane
And seeing mostly shadows
As one gropes for the words that come next!

In Times of Widespread Evil

What a pretty madhouse on top of that hill!
Like a many-layered wedding cake floating away.

The wrought-iron fence has its spikes
Lovingly sharpened by unknown wards of the
    state.

Late in the season of hunters and their dogs,
The old elms making wild, tragic gestures in the
    wind.

You can plainly see how classy the place is.
The Hindu doctor swims naked in the heart-
    shaped pool.

Mothers of the children who spit at the ceiling
Bringing roasted chickens and candy on Sunday.

The professor of dead languages
Is showing us his empty cigar clipper.

The crow, too, in the coat of the old-clothes
    dealer,
Trembling, trembling by the heavily chained gate.

Tidbit

He stuck his nose
Into the evening paper.
Got to have my glasses.
Where did I put them?

Where you left them,
Said she. Go shuffle
In the dark, grope
On table and sofa.

Not thinking to turn on
The lights. Save,
Save's all I hear,
Hard of hearing as I am.

Well, mister, I give up!
Both of them at a loss,
What next? And the paper
Sliding, sliding to the floor.

Outside a Dirtroad Trailer

O exegetes, somber hermeneuts,
Ingenious untanglers of ambiguities,
A bald little man was washing
The dainty feet of a very fat woman.

In a chair under a soaring shade tree,
She kept giggling and shaking her huge breasts.
There was also a boy with glasses
Engrossed in a book of serious appearance.

One black sock drying on the line,
A parked hearse with trash cans in the back,
And a large flag hanging limp from the pole
On a day as yet unproclaimed as a holiday.

Strong Boy

Lifting dumbbells for all to see
On his mother's front porch.
The old woman noncommittal,
Wiping her hands on her apron.

The marvel of it, think, think!
All the known and unknown gravities,
The sheer heft of the imponderables,
And he ain't about to let go.

The Quality of Light

You worship a few oblique truths,
You remind yourself on a morning
So clear you do not recognize the day
You're in a circle of things you call your own.

They measure you, themselves a bit too inanimate
To be real. And this harsh light,
One could speak of it as of a precise instrument.
Better not to ask whose it is.

You understand, you tell yourself, the rituals.
That's why you put on the black overcoat,
And open a black umbrella inside the house,
And sit at this unsteady, round table,

For the usual breakfast of mushrooms,
Which they say got so black and poisonous-
        looking
While you slept naked in the arms of
Some much-aged, big-assed Ariadne.

Dear Helen

There's a thing in the world
Called a sea cucumber.
I know nothing about it.
It just sounds cold and salty.
I think a salad of such cukes
Would be fine today.
I would have to dive for it, though,
Deep into the treacherous depths
While you mince the garlic
And sip the white wine
Into which the night is falling.
I should be back soon
With those lovely green vegetables
Out of the shark-infested sea.

Ancient Engines and Beasts

A very old horse in an old people's home.
(That's the way it looks.) Someone
Ought to ride him while the nurses
Bathe the dying. Someone tall and gaunt
Like Don Quixote. Perhaps even
With a wide-brimmed black hat to greet
The poplars twisting in the wind.
(That's the way it looks.) In the rain
They won't hear its hooves. The rider
With a pointy gray beard next to a tower
Of rusted cars. I want him to wade
Into that wide nightlike river. Smokestacks
On the other bank. Smoke billowing.
The horse asleep as he stands in the rain.
A tall rider in a pale hospital shirt
Placing his hand over his heart.
The writing on the warehouse wall calling:
Tabu. Sphinx. Solus. Maria Dolores.

To Helen

Tomorrow early I'm going to the doctor
In the blue suit and shirt you ironed.
Tomorrow I'm having my bones photographed
With my heart in its spiked branches.

It will look like a bird's nest in autumn
On a bleak day, one foot into the evening.
The tree is ill-shapen and alone in a field.
It must have been an apple, a crab apple

Tough and sour to make each tooth sore,
So that one goes off regretting, for now
The road's dark and there are new worries,
Fast swerving cars without headlights on,

Unknown drivers asleep at the wheel.
Because it's such a fine bone-chilling night.
Shadowy women are stirring black coffee,
Or they come out on the road to wait,

Wind-twisted and exquisitely blurred
In the wake of these cars that are moving
So fast or so slow, one barely hears them.
They're like clouds, if you hear them, the dark
        clouds.

Trees in the Open Country

FOR JIM

Like those who were eyewitnesses
To an enormity
And have since remained downcast
At the very spot,

Their shadows gradually lengthening
Into what look like canes, badly charred,
No choice but to lean on them eventually,
Together, and in a kind of reverie,

Awaiting the first solitary quip
From the maddeningly occulted birds,
Night birds bestirring themselves at last—
If you are still listening,

One has the impression the world
Is adamant on a matter of great importance,
And then—it isn't anymore . . .
Unless it's now the leaves' turn to reply?

Three

Painters of Angels and Seraphim

After a long lunch of roast lamb
And many heavy glasses of heavy red wine,
I fell asleep in a rowboat
That I never got around to untie
From its mooring under the willows
That went on fussing over my head
As if to make my shade even deeper.

I woke once to pull my shirt off,
And once when I heard my name
Called by a woman, distant and worried,
Since it was past sundown,
The water reflecting the dark hills,
And the sky of that chill blue
That used to signify a state of grace.

The Ant and the Bird

In those far-off days they told time
By watching ants. Eyes and ears to the ground,
They'd follow a single specimen
As it made its mysterious rounds.

When it carried its heavy loads,
When it stopped to rest for a while,
They remained just as they were:
Eyes closing, afraid to breathe,

Their shirts and dresses unbuttoned
Because of the heat. Young breasts
Never to bud further, scraggly beards
Never to be cut by a razor.

The hermit thrush perhaps wanted to sing,
But it sat mute deep in the woods.
It sat and sat as the sun forgot to set.
Then it made one solitary note.

Henri Rousseau's Bed

I took my bed into the forest.
How peaceful, I thought,
when the full moon came out.
The white stag nibbled my pillow,

the night bird sang in the hand
of the huge hairy ape.
It was not the bird of paradise.
It was a gypsy with a mandolin.

I had to run naked with my bed,
knock at the prison gate,
ask for their darkest solitary.
They obliged, rats and all. . . .

The executioner's lovely daughter
came to visit on tiptoes.
Sad bread she brought, the world's saddest.
Her beauty bandaged my eyes.

No small feat to get that bed
out of there on insomnia's bicycle.
Like a worm crossing the Brooklyn Bridge,
I found myself in a philosopher's kitchen.

It was cold and white as at the Pole.
Snow kept falling into empty pots.
I could have used a team of dogs
to pull my bed, a queue of sleepwalkers. . . .

At the late movies where I found myself next,
bedded under the screen,
the great Egyptian-style theater empty,
one could hear the wind between stars.

In the picture, a lonely veiled woman
clutched a handkerchief to her breast.
Are you the gypsy, I shouted?
And if so, where's your mandolin?

No, she replied. I'm the executioner's lovely
        daughter.
I'm on my way to the Galápagos Islands.
I need tortoise glasses to look for my love
who is asleep in the dark forest.

Silent Child

He steals a hair
From the sleeping god.
It used to fall
Over the angry eye.

Dark wet hair
In the palm of his hand
As if just bitten
By the thundering mouth.

O silent one!
In faded blue overalls
On the rickety porch
Of a grand old house.

October Arriving

I only have a measly ant
To think with today.
Others have pictures of saints,
Others have clouds in the sky.

The winter might be at the door,
For he's all alone
And in a hurry to hide.
Nevertheless, unable to decide

He retraces his steps
Several times and finds himself
On a huge blank wall
That has no window.

Dark masses of trees
Cast their mazes before him,
Only to erase them next
With a sly, sea-surging sound.

Ancient Autumn

Is that foolish youth still sawing
The good branch he's sitting on?
Do the orchard and hill wheeze because of it,
And the few remaining apples sway?
Can he see the village in the valley
The way a chicken hawk would?

Already the pale plumes of woodsmoke scatter.
The days are getting short and chilly.
Even he must rest from time to time,
So he's lit a long-stemmed pipe
To watch a chimney sweep at work
And a woman pin diapers on the line
And then go behind some bushes,
Hike her skirts so that a bit of whiteness shows,
While on the commons humpbacked men
Roll a barrel of hard cider or beer,
And still beyond, past grazing cattle
Children play soldiers and march in step.

He figures, if the wind changes direction
He'll hear them shouting commands,
But it doesn't, so the black horseman
On the cobble of the road remains inaudible.
One instant he seems to be coming,
In the next to be leaving forever in a hurry. . . .

It's these dumb shows with their vague lessons
That make him thoughtful and melancholy.
He's not even aware that he has resumed sawing,
That the big red sun is about to set.

Against Whatever It Is
That's Encroaching

Best of all is to be idle,
And especially on a Thursday,
And to sip wine while studying the light:
The way it ages, yellows, turns ashen
And then hesitates forever
On the threshold of the night
That could be bringing the first frost.

It's good to have a woman around just then,
And two is even better.
Let them whisper to each other
And eye you with a smirk.
Let them roll up their sleeves and unbutton their
        shirts a bit
As this fine old twilight deserves,

And the small schoolboy
Who has come home to a room almost dark
And now watches wide-eyed
The grownups raise their glasses to him,
The giddy-headed, red-haired woman
With eyes tightly shut,
As if she were about to cry or sing.

First Frost

The time of the year for the mystics.
October sky and the Cloud of Unknowing.
The routes of eternity beckoning.
Sign and enigma in the humblest of things.

Master cobbler Jakob Boehme
Sat in our kitchen all morning.
He sipped tea and warned of the quiet
To which the wise must school themselves.

The young woman paid no attention.
Hair fallen over her eyes,
Breasts loose and damp in her robe,
Stubbornly scrubbing a difficult stain.

Then the dog's bark brought us all outdoors,
And that wasn't just geese honking,
But Dame Julian of Norwich herself discoursing
On the marvelous courtesy and homeliness of the
    Maker.

Promises of Leniency
and Forgiveness

Orphanage in the rain,
Empty opera house with its lights dimmed,
Thieves' market closed for the day,
O evening sky with your cloudy tableaus!

Incurable romantics marrying eternal grumblers.
Life haunted by its more beautiful sister-life—
Always, always . . . we had nothing
But the way with words. Someone rising to
        eloquence

After a funeral, or in the naked arms of a woman
Who has her head averted because she's crying,
And doesn't know why. Some hairline fracture of
        the soul
Because of these razor-backed hills, bare trees and
        bushes,

Sea-blackened rocks inscrutable as card
        players . . .
One spoke then of the structure of the inquirer
        himself,
Of blues in my bread, of great works and little
        faith.
Above the clouds the firm No went on pacing.

The woman had a tiny smile and an open
        umbrella,

Since now it had started to rain in a whisper,
The kind of rain that must have whispered in
    some other life
Of which we know nothing anymore except

That someone kept watching it come down softly,
Already soot-colored to make them think of
Serious children at play, and of balls of lint in a
    dark dark corner
Like wigs, fright wigs for the infinite.

Caravan

Geese know, over such wide plains
Someone has been sent into exile.
They flee, surely, at the thought of it.
Their beaks stay firmly shut.
The trees make as if to follow them on foot,
Wielding their crutches.
Then the earth begins to unveil
Its roadside attractions.
A great many feverishly kneaded stone-likenesses
Lie in wait for the unsuspecting.
They might be shadow puppets?

The Traveling Theater of my Insomnia
Has the Honor of Presenting:
The sandbound capital of X,
Its towers that once reached to the morning star.
Archers of cosmic solitude
Welcoming us in their sights . . .
Better them than these endless plains,
Their famous mind-chilling winds
And long-tailed comets
Like a dropped litter of white mice.

The silence of dressmakers,
Cake-decorators ahead. The silence of
Lonely hearts clubs.
Dead babies with lips painted.
In X, there are work gloves,
Hearing aids, surgical dressings.
There are fireworks supplies,

Theatrical hats, beauty marks.
There's someone in a house of cards
Naked on a love seat with a tiger rug
Who'll take us under her wing.

Birthday Star Atlas

Wildest dream, Miss Emily,
Then the coldly dawning suspicion—
Always at the loss—come day
Large black birds overtaking men who sleep in
     ditches.

A whiff of winter in the air. Sovereign blue,
Blue that stands for intellectual clarity
Over a street deserted except for a far-off dog,
A police car, a light at the vanishing point

For the children to solve on the blackboard
     today—
Blind children at the school you and I know
     about.
Their gray nightgowns creased by the north wind;
Their fingernails bitten from time immemorial.

We're in a long line outside a dead-letter office.
We're dustmice under a conjugal bed carved with
     exotic fishes and monkeys.
We're in a slow-drifting coalbarge huddled
     around the television set
Which has a wire coat hanger for an antenna.

A quick view (by satellite) of the polar regions
Maternally tucked in for the long night.
Then some sort of interference—parallel lines
Like the ivory-boned needles of your
     grandmother knitting our fates together.

All things ambiguous and lovely in their
        ambiguity,
Like the nebulae in my new star atlas—
Pale ovals where the ancestral portraits have been
        taken down.
The gods with their goatees and their faint smiles

In company of their bombshell spouses,
Naked and statuesque as if entering a death camp.
They smile, too, stroke the Triton wrapped
        around the mantle clock
When they are not showing the whites of their
        eyes in theatrical ecstasy.

Nostalgias for the theological vaudeville.
A false springtime cleverly painted on cardboard
For the couple in the last row to sigh over
While holding hands which unknown to them

Flutter like bird-shaped scissors. . . .
Emily, the birthday atlas!
I kept turning its pages awed
And delighted by the size of the unimaginable;

The great nowhere, the everlasting nothing—
Pure and serene doggedness
For the hell of it—and love,
Our nightly stroll the color of silence and time.

Without a Sough of Wind

Against the backdrop
Of a twilight world
In which one has done so little
For one's soul

She hangs a skirt
On the doorknob
She puts a foot on the chair
To take off a black stocking

And it's good to have eyes
Just then for the familiar
Large swinging breasts
And the cleft of her ass

Before the recital
Of that long day's
Woes and forebodings
In the warm evening

With the drone of insects
On the window screen
And the lit dial of a radio
Providing what light there is

Its sound turned much too low
To make out the words
Of what could be
A silly old love song